RUBY'S KITCHEN

RECIPES OF GREAT TASTES

ARUNDHATI SENGUPTA

Contents

Foreword

Cooking has been regarded as one of the greatest arts right from the time of Julius Caesar. Although elements of the art of cooking are easy to define, I have discovered over the years that the tastes which still linger on my tongue are the tastes that mattered. In that respect, my nanny still remains unbeatable as the greatest cook in my life. We called her 'Nannabhai' derived from the Bengali word 'ranna' for cooking. Be it a simple Hilsa egg fry or peas pulao or stuffed chicken or quail (bauter) roast, mutton, or chicken stew the food always used to be a gastronomical delight. My mother inherited some of her skills and tickled our senses with dishes like Tomato fish, Mutton kofta curry, and Pudding. Now it's my wife who has mastered the art of tickling my senses. Her talent for improvisation has created a new type of Shammi Kebab which is a fusion of Lucknow Shammi Kebab and Tunda Kebab. The effort has paid her – like the saying goes a man's heart is through his stomach. Cooking has been regarded as one of the greatest arts right from the time of Julius Caesar. Although elements of the art of cooking are easy to define, I have discovered over the years that the tastes which still linger on my tongue are the tastes that mattered. In that respect, my nanny still remains unbeatable as the greatest cook in my life. We called her 'nannabhai' derived from the Bengali word 'ranna' for cooking. Be it a simple Hilsa egg fry or peas pulao or stuffed chicken or quail (bauter) roast, mutton, or chicken stew the food always used to be a gastronomical delight. My mother inherited some of her skills and tickled our senses with dishes like Tomato fish, Mutton kofta curry, and Pudding. Now it's my wife who has mastered the art of tickling my senses. Her talent for improvisation has created a new type of Shammi Kebab which is a fusion of Lucknow Shammi Kebab and Tunda Kebab. The effort has paid her – like the saying goes a man's heart is through his stomach. The book is on a collection of recipes from my wife's (Ruby's) kitchen.

Biswajit Sengupta, Chartered Engineer & LightingConsultant; Email:biswajitsengupta2006@gmail.com Website: https://www.ranaruby.in; *3C Mayukh,68/3 Pratapaditya Road,Calcutta 700026,India*

FRIED SARDINE

FRIED SARDINE - More on 'GREAT TASTES

From Ruby's Kitchen

SARDINE FRY

Ingredients

Fish – 2 whole pcs (medium size)

Ginger Paste – 1 tsp

Onion Paste – 1 tbsp

Black Pepper(crushed) – 1 tbsp

Olive Oil – 1.5 tbsp

Parsley (finely chopped) – 1 tbsp

Salt – 1.5 tbsp

Vinegar - 1 tbsp

Lemon – 2 pcs

Besan – half tsp

Capsicum, tomato, cauliflower, beans - all chopped into tiny cubes

Method of Preparation.

Clean fish and keep it soaked for about one hour in vinegar, lemon juice (two medium-sized fresh lemons), and 1 tablespoon salt. After that wash, thoroughly dry the fish with a towel napkin. Marinate the fish with onion paste, ginger paste, salt, and parsley, preferably for about two hours. Once marinated, apply a thin layer of Besan coating on the entire fish. Then place the fish on one table, spoon oil on a frying pan, cover it with a lid and let it fry on low flame for 10 minutes. Next, flip the fish to the other side, apply half a teaspoon of black pepper and continue the frying process for 10 minutes. After that turn, the fish again, use the rest of the black pepper on the exposed side, raise the flame, place all vegetables in the frying pan and fry each side of the fish for two minutes. Try to keep the pan covered with a lid when frying takes place. Pour the rest of the lemon juice once the frying is over, and your fried sardine is ready. Bon appétit!

The Cheesy Variation

Cover the fried fish with one tablespoon of grated Parmesan cheese and a sprinkle of crushed black pepper. Place the lid for one minute to allow the cheese to melt over the fish. Serve the dish with toast. Bon Appétit!

Fried Sardine

Mutton Rogan Josh

A Wazwan Delicacy

Ingredients:

Mutton----1/2kg

Hing (Asafetida) – 1/4 teaspoon

Cinnamon (darchini)- 2 pieces (1" each)

Clove (labanga) - 5 pieces

Black cardamom (boro elaich) - 3 pieces

Whole black pepper 1/2 teaspoon

Juice one whole large onion

coriander powder - 1 teaspoon

Cumin powder - 1 teaspoon

Ratan Jote - 1 teaspoon

Kashmiri Mirch powder – 2/3 tsp

Hung Curd 250gm

Fennel powder - 1teaspoon

Ginger powder - 2 teaspoon

Vegetable oil – 1 tablespoon

Method:

Boil 500 gm mutton in roughly 500ml water till soft and keep the stock and the mutton separately aside. Put a large pan on the gas and add oil. When the oil is hot (but not smoking) add the whole garam masalas and black pepper. When the spices start popping, add the meat, and then slowly add the onion juice. Stir fry on low heat. When meat becomes almost dry and the onion juice has been completely absorbed, add hung curd, coriander powder, cumin powder, fennel powder, asafetida, ginger powder, Kashmiri chili powder, and ratanjote. Keep frying on slow heat and when the mutton again becomes almost dry, add salt to taste and two pinches of sugar. Pour the entire mutton stock and let it simmer for 5-6 minutes.

Bon appetite!

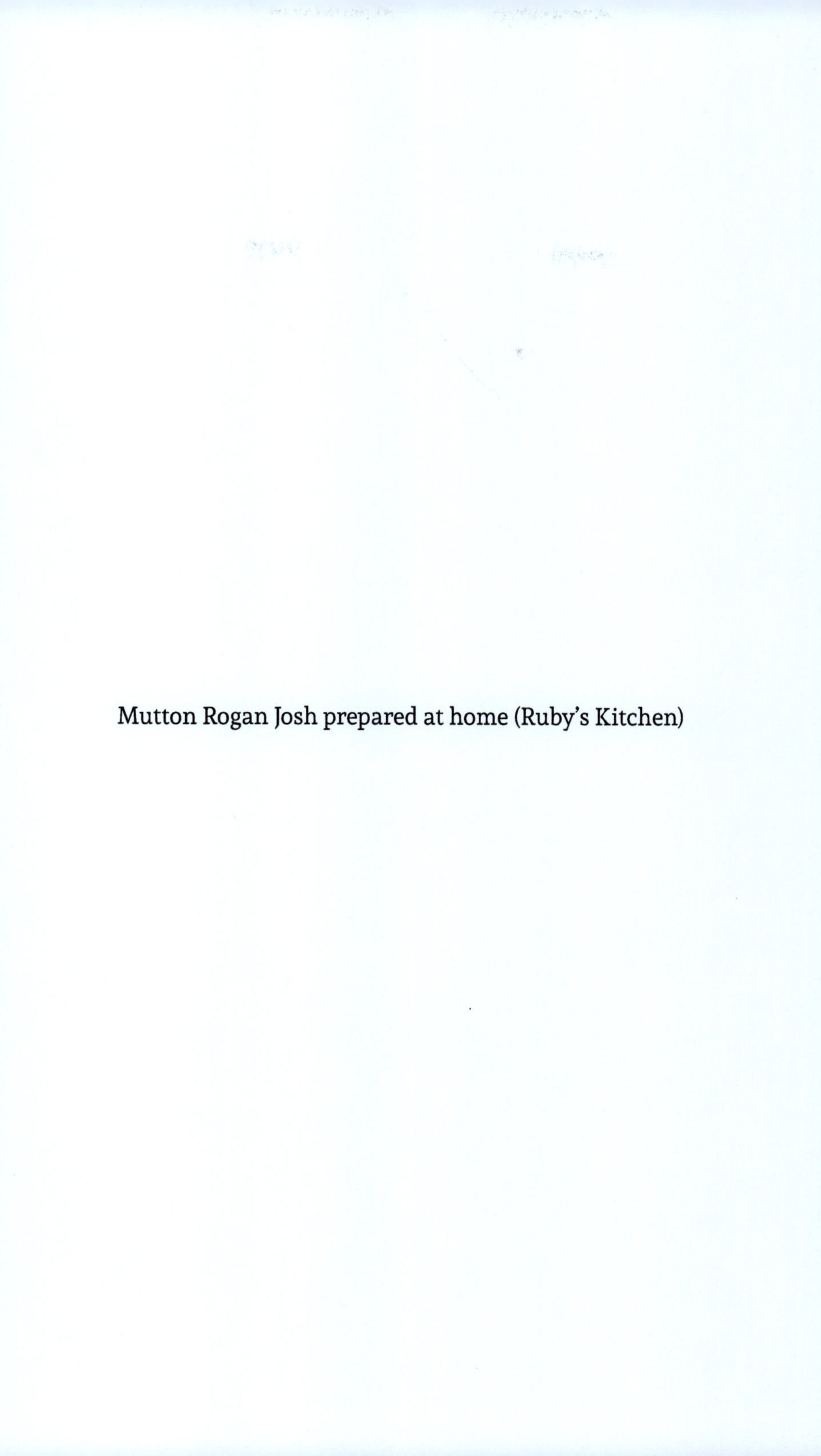

Mutton Rogan Josh prepared at home (Ruby's Kitchen)

Kashmere Chicken Curry

Wazwan Recipe

Ingredient:

750-800gm chicken

Chopped Onion – Finely chopped from 2 medium-sized onions.

Whole dry Red Chilli – 3-4

Kashmiri Chilli Powder – 2 Tsp

Garlic chopped - 6 /7 flakes

Coriander Powder – 1 Tsp

Cloves – 6/7 pcs

Cardamom – 6/7 pcs

Cinnamon – ½ pcs

Cashew nuts – 50 gm

Almonds – 25 gm

Hung Curd – 150/200 ml

Coriander leaves – approx. 1 sprig

Method :

Grind cashew nuts and almonds with the curd till it forms a paste. Marinate the chicken pieces for about half an hour in the paste.

Fry the chopped onions in a kadhai till it starts browning. Then add the dry red chilis, chili powder, and all the other ingredients except the marinated chicken. Saute for 3-4 minutes and then add the chicken. Sauté till the chicken pieces take up a deep brownish hue. Then add around 2/3 cups of water, and add salt to taste. Simmer in low heat for about half an hour. Garnish with Coriander leaves.

Bon appetite!

Kashmere Chicken Curry and rice at Prince Restaurant,Pahalgam

Gustabha

Mutton Gustabha-a delicious Wazwan meatball preparation

Ingredients:

Finely minced mutton – 1/2kg

Kashmiri Garam Masala- 2/3 tsp

Kashmiri chili powder – 2/3 Tsp

Fennel seed – 1tsp

Ginger powder – 1 Tsp

Whole black pepper – 2/3 tsp

Cardamom – 4/5 pcs

Coriander powder – 1tbsp

Khoya – half cup

Hung Curd – half cup

Milk – approx. one cup

Ghee – 2 tbsp

Method:

Make a smooth paste with the Kashmiri chili powder, fennel powder, ginger powder, coriander powder, garam masala, minced meat, a little curd, and ghee. Then form balls of around 2-inch diameter. Heat the ghee and add Khoya, curd, garam masala, and salt to taste. Pour the milk after some time and then add the Koftas. Simmer in low heat till the liquid evaporates partly. Each Gustabha meatball is quite giant in size and soft after it is cooked. Suggest slicing each ball into four equal segments to savor it with plain rice, tandoori roti, or naan.

Bon appetite!

Mutton Gustabha garnished with coriander leaves (prepared at Ahdoos Srinagar)

Mutton Rista

Mutton Kofta - Wazwan style

Ingredients:

Ratan Jote – 1 cup

Saffron soaked in water – approx. one cup

Kashmiri Chilli powder – ½ tsp

Ginger powder – 1 Tsp

Cardamom – 4/5 pcs

Fennel powder – 2tsp

Cinnamon sticks – 2/3 pcs

Cloves – 3/ 4 pcs

Hing – roughly a pinch

Bay leaves

Method:

Make around one-inch balls from minced meat after mixing cardamom powder, a little salt, and one tsp ginger powder. When the oil gets heated, add all the ingredients except the koftas, saffron, and ratan jote. After a few minutes add the keema balls and stir-fry gently till the Koftas turn reddish brown. Then add saffron soaked in water and a cup of Ratan jote. Add salt to taste and simmer on low heat for around ten minutes. The Koftas after cooking should have a characteristic rubbery bite in contrast to Gustabha where the meatballs are soft and melt in the mouth. Best served with plain rice or roti.

Bon appetite!

Mutton Rista prepared in Gulmarg

Recipe of Sorshe Ilish

Recipe of Shorshe Ilish - Dhaka's delight

(Hilsa Fish in mustard sauce)

Ingredients

4 Ilish pieces

50 gm hung curd

4 green chilies

1 tbsp ground mustard

1/2 tsp turmeric powder

1/2 tsp cashmere mirch(chili) powder

2 tbsp mustard oil

salt to taste

2 pinches of sugar

1/2 cup water

Method

Mix all the ingredients together with Ilish pieces in a kadhai. Cover with a lid and slow cook in medium flame for 10 minutes, give 10 minutes standing time. Serve hot with rice & gandharaj lebu(a special aromatic lemon available in Bengal in abundance) on the banana leaf.

Caution: Do not fry the fish pieces.

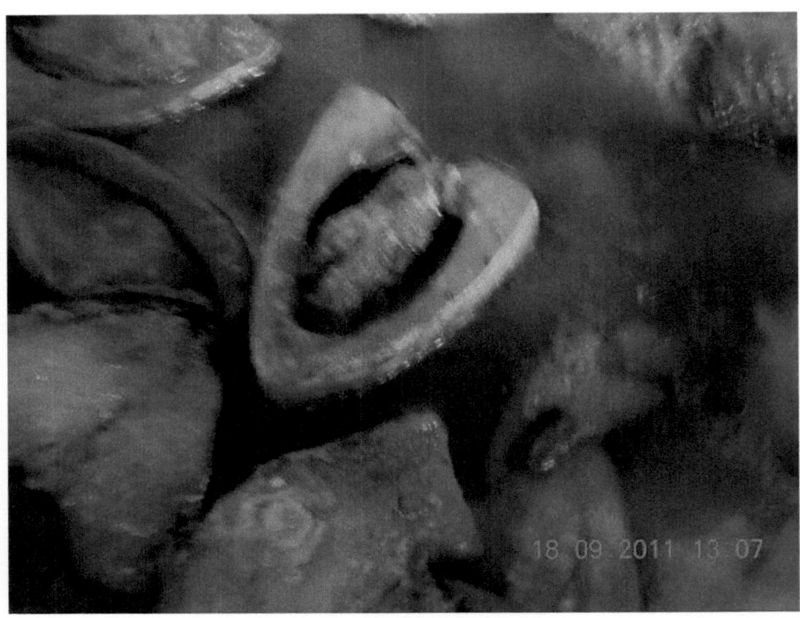

Sorshe Ilish prepared at Ruby;s Kitchen

Mutton Kofta Curry

Recipe of Mutton Kofta Curry (as prepared in Ruby's Kitchen)

Ingredients

1/2 kg finely minced meat

200g hung curd

1 tsp finely chopped onion

2 green chilies chopped into small pieces

1 tbsp chopped coriander leaves

salt to taste

Method

For the gravy

250gm onion paste.25 gm ginger paste, 10 garlic pod paste.200gm hung curd.

Mix all the ingredients with minced meat with 200gm hung curd and marinate for one hour. Heat oil and then add 1 tsp sugar for caramelization, 2 pcs cloves, and 2 pcs cardamom.1pc cinnamon Then adds garlic, onion, and ginger paste and sauté in a pan till onions turn brown. Add 200g curd and keep stirring. Add water and salt to taste. When the curry starts boiling, make medium-sized meatballs manually and add them to the gravy one by one. Cook in low flame for 15 minutes. Give standing time 15 minutes. Serve hot.

Mutton Kofa Curry (on left) & Aloo Dum (on right)

Mutton Shami Kebab

Shami Kebab- the taste of Oudh

Ingredients

Mutton Keema - 500 gms

Chana Dal (pulse)- 1 cup

Turmeric powder- 1/2 tsp

Garlic - 10 to 12 cloves

Ginger (grated) - 2 tbsp

Onion (medium size, slit into two) - 4 pcs

Cloves - 10 pcs

Fennel seeds (saunf) - 1 tsp

Cumin (jeera white) - 1 tbsp

Coriander - 1 tbsp

Cardamom (large) - 2 pcs

Cardamom (small) - 4 pcs

Cinnamon (2 inch sticks) - 2 pcs

Nutmeg - 1 small pc

Poppy seed - 1 tbsp

Method

Stage 1: Set Aside the following:

- *Chana Dal (pulse) - 1 cup preferably 5 to 6 hrs*
- *Small pcs of onions (sliced from 2 medium-sized onions),4 deseeded green*

chilies, a bunch of coriander leaves to be kept soaked in lime juice from one medium-sized lemon.

- *Beaten egg (from one egg)*

Stage 2:

Mutton keema and all ingredients will be boiled in 2 cups of water on low flame for 20/25 minutes till water dries out.

Stage 3:

The boiled keema, chana dal, small pcs of cubed onions deseeded green chilies, and coriander leaves are to be poured into a mixer grinder or preferably a 'shi pata' for manual grinding. Manual grinding enhances the fineness of the kebab. A dough is to be prepared after combining the mix with the beaten egg for tighter

cohesion.

Stage 4:

Half a tsp of rose water (optional) to be mixed with the dough for added taste. A kebab's shape and size must be drawn from the dough and grilled on a Tawa.

The kebabs prepared on the Tawa can be served with roti, finely sliced onions,green chilis (whole), and pudina coriander chutney

Bon Apetit

Shami Kebab prepared at Ruby's Kitchen - *Lucknowi type*

Malai Prawn with 'Gandhoraj' Lemon

Malai Prawn - Bengal's Prawn delicacy

Ingredients

Prawns (large) - 500 gm

Onion paste - 2 tbsp

Deseeded green chili paste - 1 tsp

Ginger paste - 1 tbsp

Cooking oil - 3 tbsp

Coconut milk - 200 ml tetra pack

Sugar - 1/2 tsp

Gandhoraj lebu (lemon) - 1 pc

Gandhoraj lebu leaves - 4/5 pcs

Method

Normally, the preparation time takes about 20 minutes and the cooking time about 15 minutes.

- Wash and clean the prawn pieces; apply turmeric and salt on the pieces and then set them aside.
- Pour three tablespoons of oil into a pan or 'kadhai'. Heat it and then stir 1/2 teaspoon sugar till it turns brownish.
- Pour the onion paste, simmer for 3/4 minutes, and then add ginger paste and green chili paste. Saute till the mixture almost dries. Add salt to taste, and after 2/3 minutes place the prawns. Stir both sides of the prawns in the mixture for 2 to 3 minutes. The prawns will turn pink. Place the 'Gonghoraj lebu leaves' and continue stirring for 2/3 minutes.
- Next, pour coconut milk, and boil on slow flame for 3 to 4 minutes.
- When the preparation cools down a little, sprinkle 'Gondhoraj lebu', stir and cover.

The prepared dish can be served with rice.

Bon Apetit.

Malai Prawn with Gondhoraj Lebu (***prepared at Ruby's Kitchen*****)**

Printed by Libri Plureos GmbH in Hamburg,
Germany

9 798887 838847